STECK-VAU[illegible]

NEW WA[illegible]

HEADS and TAILS

Sorry, Sam!

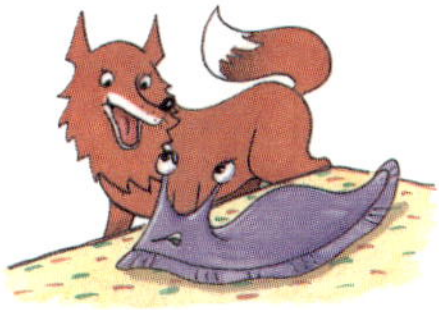

STECK-VAUGHN COMPANY

A Division of Harcourt Brace & Company

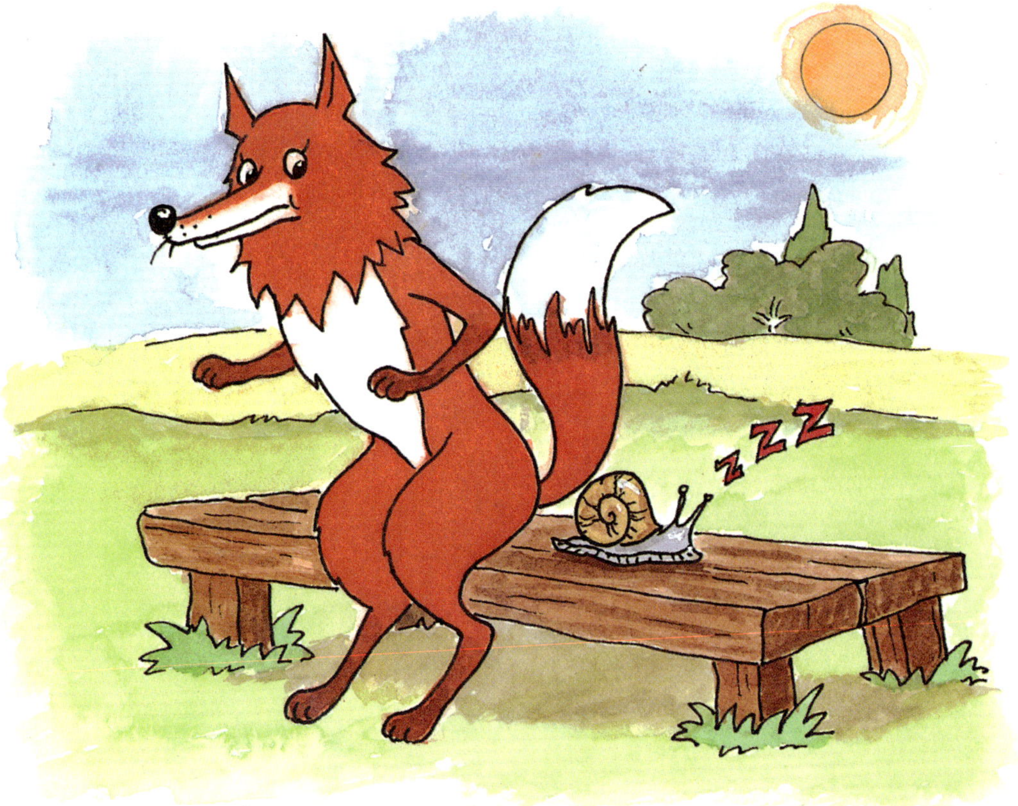

Sam sat on a snail.

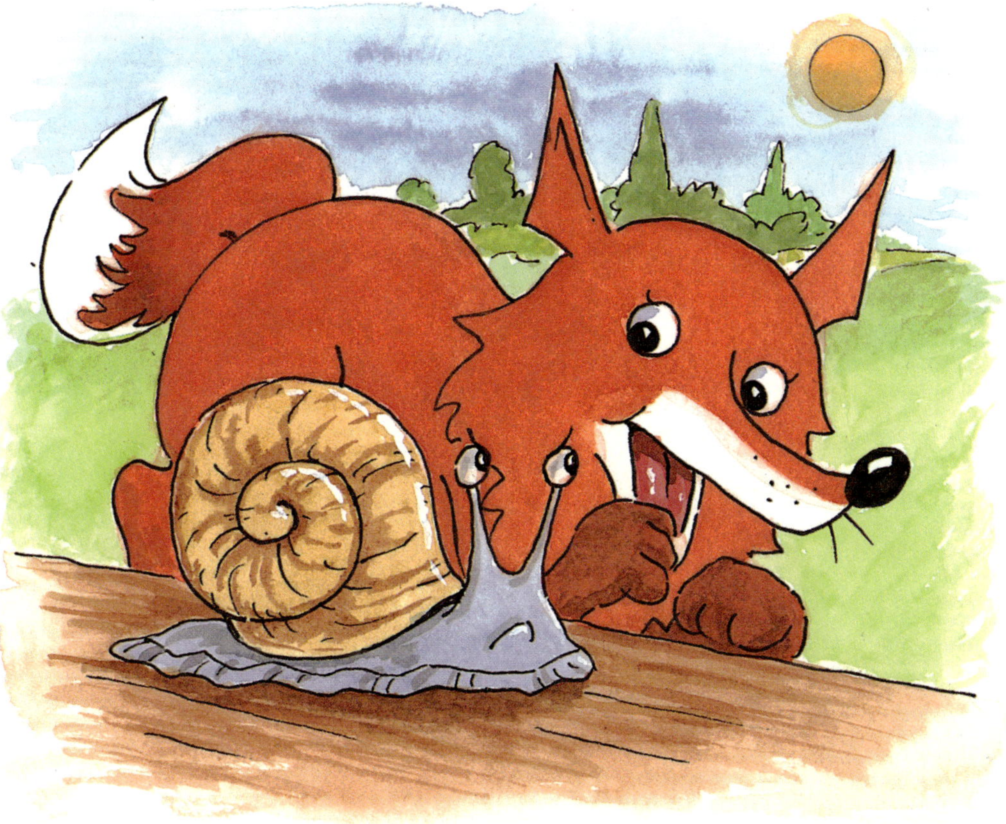

Sorry, snail!

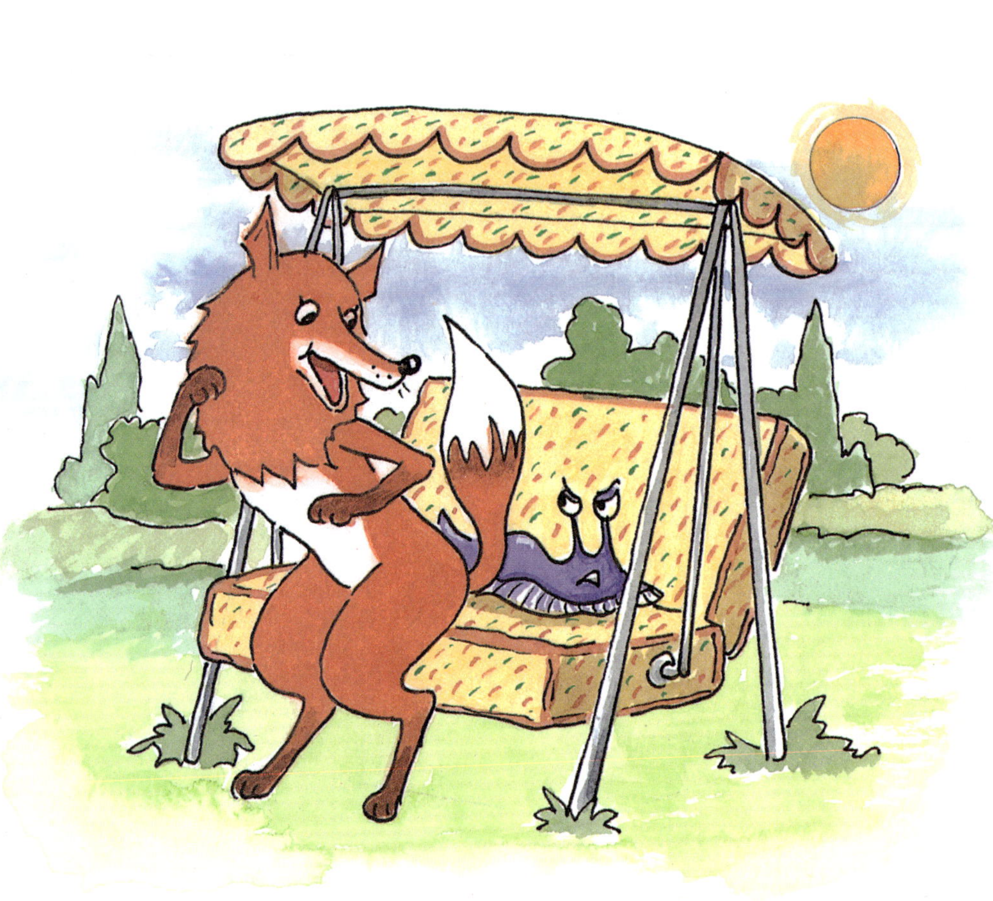

Sam sat on a slug.

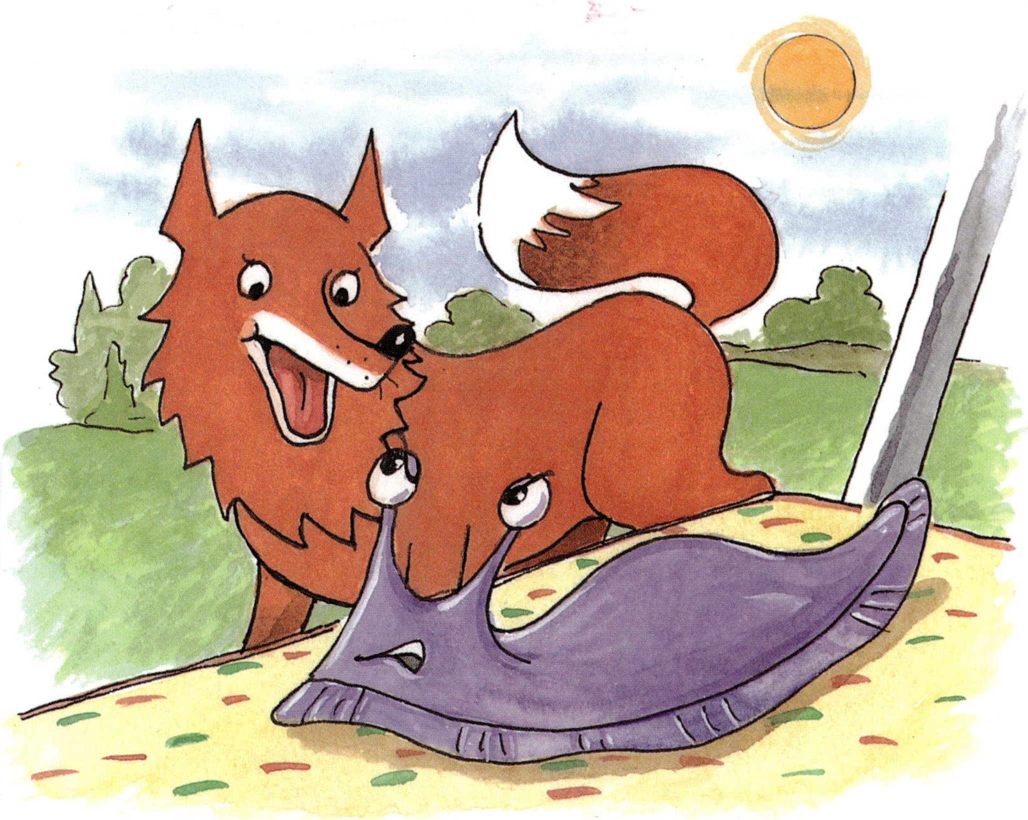

Sorry, slug!

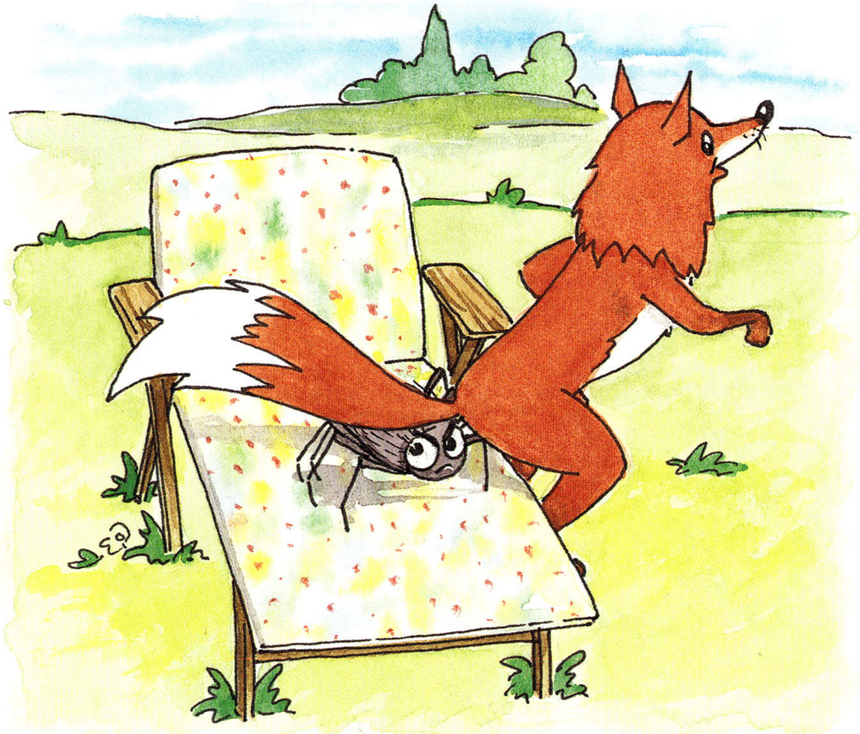

Sam sat on a spider.

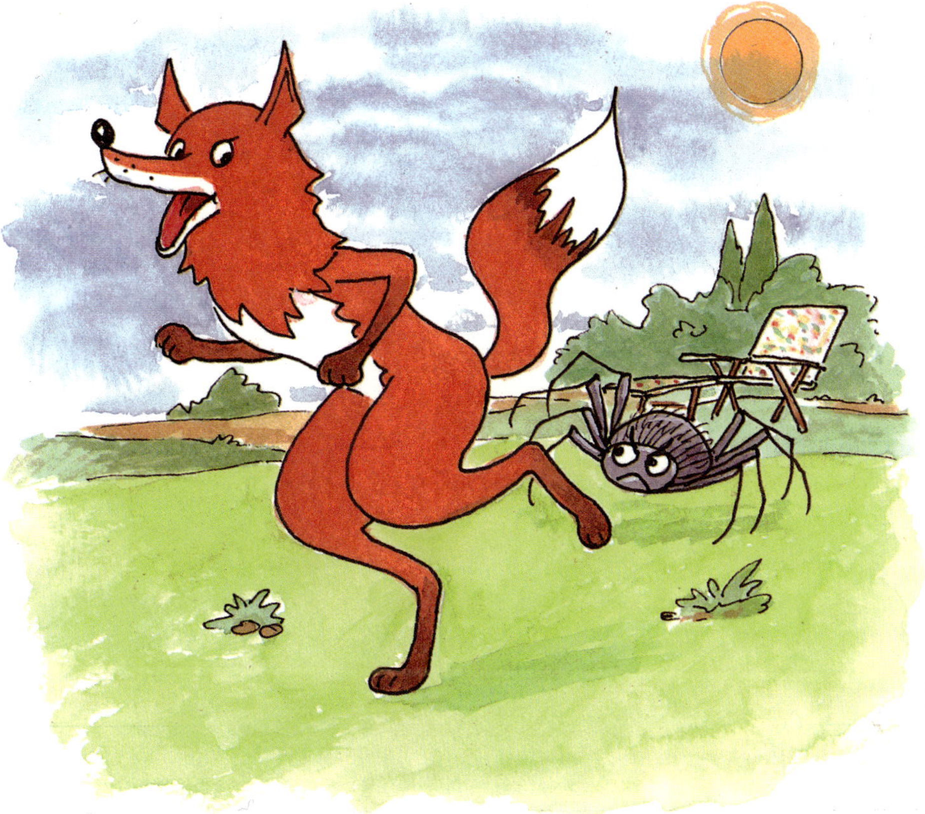

That stings!

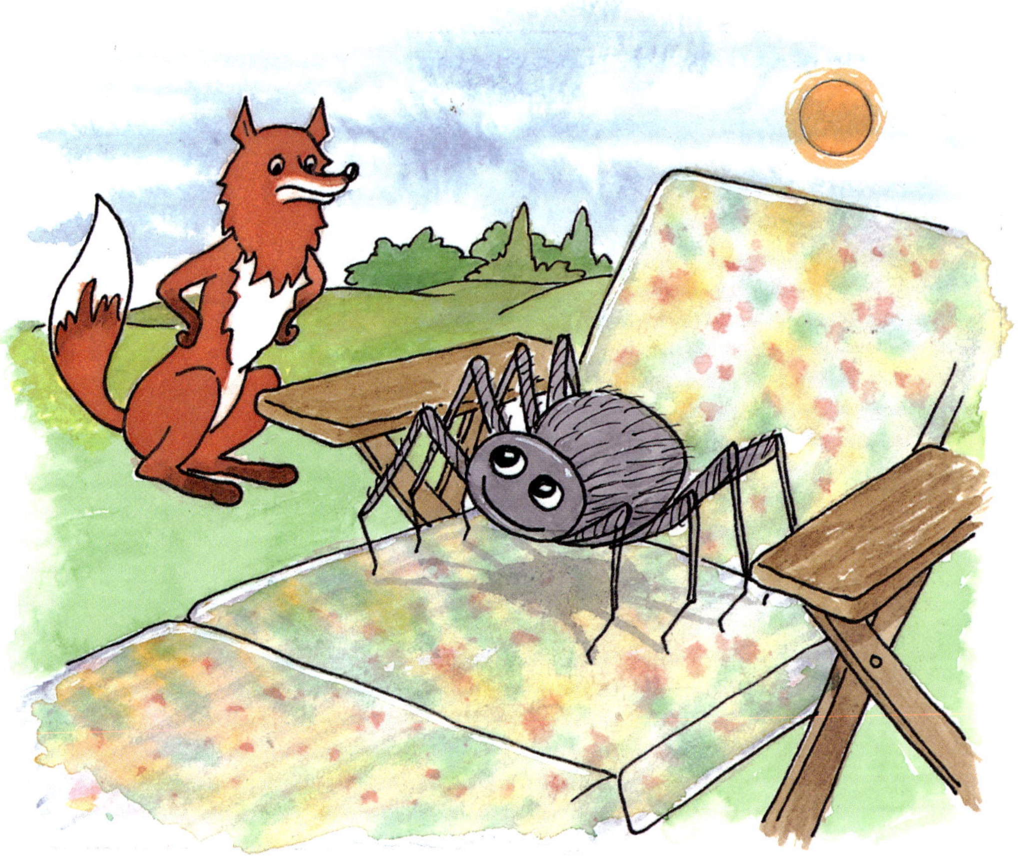

Sorry, Sam!